MW01050417

SandCastle

Sight Words

There Are Ants Down There!

Kelly Doudna

Consulting Editor Monica Marx, M.A./Reading Specialist

ABDO
Publishing Company

Published by SandCastle™, an imprint of ABDO Publishing Company, 4940 Viking Drive, Edina, Minnesota 55435.

Printed in the United States.

Credits
Edited by: Pam Price
Curriculum Coordinator: Nancy Tuminelly
Cover and Interior Design and Production: Mighty Media
Photo Credits: Corbis Images, Digital Vision, Eyewire Images, PhotoDisc, Stockbyte

Library of Congress Cataloging-in-Publication Data

Doudna, Kelly, 1963-
    There are ants down there! / Kelly Doudna.
        p. cm. -- (Sight words)
    Includes index.
    Summary: Uses simple sentences, photographs, and a brief story to introduce six different words: are, down, her, is, know, there.
    ISBN 1-59197-473-9
    1. Readers (Primary) 2. Vocabulary--Juvenile literature. [1. Reading.] I. Title. II. Series.

PE1119.D68635 2003
428.1--dc21
                                                                        2003050313

SandCastle™ books are created by a professional team of educators, reading specialists, and content developers around five essential components that include phonemic awareness, phonics, vocabulary, text comprehension, and fluency. All books are written, reviewed, and leveled for guided reading, early intervention reading, and Accelerated Reader® programs and designed for use in shared, guided, and independent reading and writing activities to support a balanced approach to literacy instruction.

Let Us Know

After reading the book, SandCastle would like you to tell us your stories about reading. What is your favorite page? Was there something hard that you needed help with? Share the ups and downs of learning to read. We want to hear from you! To get posted on the ABDO Publishing Company Web site, send us e-mail at:

sandcastle@abdopub.com

SandCastle Level: Beginning

Featured Sight Words

are   down

her   is

know   there

are

Jill and John are camping with their parents.

Rosa puts her plate down on her lap.

Mia fishes with her mom.

Mark is getting ready to fish.

Ted and Jay know
how to fish with a net.

There is a little campfire.

Down at the Campground

Holly, Trish, Matt, and Kay know each other.

They are sitting down.

Holly puts her marshmallow on a stick.

There are enough for everybody.

The plate of marshmallows is on the ground.

Oh no! There are ants down there!

More Sight Words in This Book

a	on
and	other
at	the
for	their
how	they
little	to
no	with
of	

All words identified as sight words in this book are from Edward Bernard Fry's "First Hundred Instant Sight Words."

Picture Index

ants, p. 20

campfire, p. 15

marshmallow, p. 18

net, p. 13

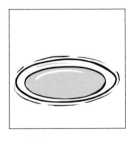

plate, pp. 7, 20

stick, p. 18

About SandCastle™

A professional team of educators, reading specialists, and content developers created the SandCastle™ series to support young readers as they develop reading skills and strategies and increase their general knowledge. The SandCastle™ series has four levels that correspond to early literacy development in young children. The levels are provided to help teachers and parents select the appropriate books for young readers.

Emerging Readers
(no flags)

Beginning Readers
(1 flag)

Transitional Readers
(2 flags)

Fluent Readers
(3 flags)

These levels are meant only as a guide. All levels are subject to change.

To see a complete list of SandCastle™ books and other nonfiction titles from ABDO Publishing Company, visit **www.abdopub.com** or contact us at:

4940 Viking Drive, Edina, Minnesota 55435 • 1-800-800-1312 • fax: 1-952-831-1632